DRAT!

being the encapsulated view of life
by W. C. Fields in his own words

Edited by Richard J. Anobile

Introduction by Ed McMahon

AN NAL BOOK
THE WORLD PUBLISHING COMPANY
NEW YORK   CLEVELAND

First Printing, August, 1968

Published by The New American Library, Inc.
in association with
The World Publishing Company
2231 West 110th Street, Cleveland, Ohio

Library of Congress Catalog Card Number: 68-56966

Printed in the United States of America

Contents

notes on DRAT!

It is difficult to retain or maintain perspective on any subject, let alone W. C. Fields, after having viewed nearly thirty of his films during three weekends.

I viewed the films in a livingroom: for my friends that gave me a certain cachet, an aura of prestige. Had I seen the films in a theatre, those same friends would have considered me not even a buff, but a nut.

Just that I had seen the films gave rise to, "You lucky dog." My bloodshot eyes, my general lassitude when trying to catch up on sleep, my catatonic attitude toward traffic — these counted for little, in fact were ignored by my envious friends.

Then, I had to listen to everyone's recitation of favorite lines, and accounts of favorite scenes. Not only that I had great difficulty in mustering interest in garbled anecdotes, but I had no enrgy to correct inaccurate recollections. The one thing that struck me, however, was that if you see the films of Fields one at a time and far apart, you tend to recall only the good and funny parts, and you forget the long dreary stretches, the painfully bad supporting casts, the passages of utter drivel, the films that were, as Richard Shepard says elsewhere in this book, absolute dogs. Therefore (now that I've regained some measure of stamina and vitality): "David Copperfield" is a *dog* of a film; the long and glorious single shot sequence in "It's A Gift" *does* have some dialogue but no one remembers it because the entire scene is a small masterpiece of a virtually silent Fields.

"Do you remember when . . . ?" is how most of my friends began their questioning—of my knowledge of Fields films. "Do you remember when Fields said 'Has Mickey Finn been in?' " My friend was obviously referring to the sequence in "The Bank Dick" when Fields was trying his best to incapacitate Franklin Pangborn whose mission it was to examine the bank's books. Fields dragged Pangborn into the local establishment, The Black Pussy Cat Cafe. Pangborn ordered a very light drink, but Fields coyly questioned the bartender, "Has Michael Finn been in?" The bartender and the audience got the message, and Pangborn got the lethal drink.

"Do you remember when Fields was falling in a basket and said, 'Don't worry about the last foot?' " I don't remember it that way, but as long as I'm playing twenty questions let me say that the scene in question is from "Never Give a Sucker an Even Break." Fields and Gloria Jean were making a get-away from a 2000-foot cliff in a primitive elevator — a pulley wicker basket. Gloria Jean exclaims, "Uncle Bill, we'll be killed, we're falling 2000 feet!" "Don't worry about the first 1,999 feet, dear," Fields counseled, "It's that last foot that you have to be careful of!"

"How about the time Fields said that he didn't see the horse in the back of the diner?" My friend had just butchered a very funny scene where Fields had clashed with a bitchy waitress. His actual line was "I din't squawk about the steak, I merely said I didn't see that old horse you used to have tethered out back." It was also in this scene that one of Fields' most quoted lines appears: "What's the amount of the insult?"

In preparing the book, I found that locating the films and obtaining permission from the owners was easy compared to rounding up the films for screening. Fields is enjoying a revival unmatched by any other screen comedian. His films. are in constant demand throughout the nation, especially for college campus Fields Film Festivals. Because of this, I had to screen the films on weekends, three weekends, I might mention, of unprecedented lovely sunshiney spring days.

However, once past "Mrs. Wiggs of the Cabbage Patch" Fields himself was the source of the inspiration. Respite was soon at hand, *spiritus fermenti* in the form of frozen daquiries. At eight in the morning, ending a seven-hour session of viewing, I even sounded so much like Fields that I was afraid to face my nose in a mirror.

The book in this, its final form, may reveal traces of that work routine, but a few aspects of book are a result of sober thought. The running commentary in large type beginning on page 17 is taken from an article written by Fields in a 1942 issue of Pic Magazine. Its original title was "Alcohol and Me." As you read it, you will find that it provides an index to the entire screen character of Fields. The photos are for the most part stills from his motion pictures The publicity shots have been kept to a minimum. The quotes and the stills they accompany are seldom from the same film. It was most often a case of finding (or stumbling across) happy juxtapositions of the photo and the quote. The humor of these combinations is not so unlike the frequently irreverent irrelevancy of Fields' humor. For those who *must* know, the source of each photo and each quote is listed on pages 127 and 128.

I did not laugh alone in an empty livingroom. As with all books, this volume was not a one-man operation. I should, therefore, like to thank all those who have helped in the presentation of *Drat!*

First and foremost I wish to thank Miss Jane Wagner for her invaluable assistance. She has been creatively active in all phases of this book and literally deserves the purple heart for withstanding five months of my numerous phone calls and ridiculous screening schedules — not to mention my idosyncrasies. Therefore:
JANE WAGNER, THANK YOU.

I also wish to thank Metro-Goldwyn-Mayer, and Norman Kaphan; MCA-TV, and Sal Grasso; Paramount Pictures, and Irving Adler; United World Films, and Frank Gilhaus and Maurice Sims; Universal Pictures, and Milt Livingston, Eric Nauman and Irving Weiner; the Museum of Modern Art Film Library, and Richard Corliss; Harry Chester, our talented and tolerant designer; Miss Carolyn Knowles, Otis Cribblecoblis, Charles Bogle and Mahatma Kane Jeeves.
—Richard J. Anobile

"Ah, but it's great to be alive."

by Ed McMahon

In Atlantic City, at the very beginning of his career, W. C. Fields was a professional drowner. Before an audience, gathered by wily strategy, Fields would put on a convincing show of drowning. When he had been rescued and had stepped on dry ground, he would throw back his head, thump his chest and announce expansively, "Ah, but it's great to be alive," and would lure the crowd that had gathered on to a nearby amusement pier.

In one way or another, Fields was to be the same professional drowner throughout his career. Quite wittingly, more often than not, he wades in, goes down and under. Then, after his rescue, usually effected by his own wits, he will offer the grand observation. Usually it is a remark or a gesture that on the surface seems most appropriate, yet somehow, by some little bit, it is all wrong in the light of what has really happened. Today we might call it a *put on,* but we'd have to add that in his case it is done with impeccable aplomb.

In *The Bank Dick,* for instance, Fields is walking past a man having trouble repairing an expensive automobile. Fields stops and offers experienced assistance. And for a moment you're not sure. The offer has been made with such offhand assurance. But no sooner does Fields touch the engine than it falls to the ground. Fields walks off with no lack of nonchalance, as if he had accomplished exactly what he had offered. Later in the day he again passes the man, who now has a much bigger job on his hands than he had before his first encounter with Fields. Casual, but unconcerned, Fields says, "Still at it, I see."

As The Great McGonigle, the leader of a thespian troupe in *The Old-Fashioned Way,* Fields is a fast-talking conniver who tries to hold his show together — not too successfully — by using his wits since there is no money. The group arrives by train in the town where they are to play that night. A large brass band at the station strikes up the music. Fields responds with a modest yet somehow grandiose tip of his hat. As he comes off the train, he bows right and left, walks under the arch of swords with his troupe, and out into the streets of the town. There is not a hint in his manner that he is surprised. There is absolutely nothing but regal acknowledgement of the reception, with an air that it is more than justly due The Great McGonigle and his troupe. If he had known that the band was there to greet a gaudily uniformed lodge official who stood behind him on the train platform, would he have acted differently? Perhaps he did know, but by the time he had swept past the reception line he had had not only his moment of satisfaction, but had given a moment of discomfort to everyone waiting in the station. Little matter that the reception was not for him.

It's this beautiful kind of counterpoint that you see again and again in the Fields films. The world crushes him and he crushes the world and sometimes it's all happening at once, or it's difficult, at least, to tell just who is crushing whom.

Then there's that great back porch scene in *It's a Gift*. Fields has decided to sleep on the swing, in order to escape the nagging of his wife. No sooner does he settle himself on the swing than things begin to happen. One chain holding up the swing comes loose. Fields negotiates this and settles down again to sleep. One thing after another, the milkman, the kid upstairs, Baby LeRoy, a longtime adversary, a dog, a coconut rolling erratically down several flights of back porch stairs— nothing in that little world is going to let him sleep. Yet each time that he settles down again, there's something in the way he punches the pillow and fits his head and shoulders against it that makes you wonder. Just what is it that Fields is doing to that pillow, to the world itself? It's as if he had found a little spot in the enemy that is not half so well known as the Achilles Heel, but twice as vulnerable. And most of the time he doesn't stick around to see the wince or hear the howl of pain when it registers. He just saunters on, twirling his cane. Until the cane catches in a fence and he is thrown again.

It's the flair of the man that we admire first when we watch him. But I think that the great popularity he's enjoying now — and not just with the young people, though especially with them — is because of his utter disregard of the Establishment, of the way things are properly done.

Fields in *The Man on the Flying Trapeze* gives us one wonderful scene as a memory expert in a bank. Fields has total recall about every client and potential client. In an emergency the bank president goes to Field's rolltop desk to locate an important letter. The famous filing system is exposed as a veritable mountain of paper just crammed into the desk. Only Fields can find the letter, which he does by riffling through the vast heap, muttering something like "1931, 1932 . . . Ah, yes, here it is, April 11, 1934." It's in this film, too, that in order to get time off to see a wrestling match, Fields asks for the afternoon off in order to attend his mother-in-law's funeral. When someone says sympathetically to him, "It must be hard to lose your mother-in-law," Fields drawls, "Yes, it is . . . almost impossible, in fact."

It's this total disregard of arbitrary rightness and wrongness that delights us. W. C. Fields was, perhaps, the first of the balloon busters. He stood valiantly in the face of the storm of what used to be. We talk a lot about relationships and communications today. Fields established his relationships on his own terms and he communicated. You just know that if he saw a guy selling apples on the street corner and the apple stand was held up in place only by one plucky little stick, Fields would kick that stick, just to let the guy know that no one should be so dumb as to expect one wobbly stick to do the job. More important, maybe, Fields would also feel it necessary to let the guy know that he should never believe that someone walking by wouldn't ever kick that stick and upset the applecart. Because the truth is that there are a lot of potential applecart upsetters and sooner or later one of them, like Fields, is going to come along and do it.

So when we watch the Fields movies today, or when we see David Black's Broadway musical based on the life and art of Fields, it's because we want to see Fields doing those unacceptable things that we want to do. And Fields, doing them, releases our tensions, helps relieve our anxieties. That's what great comedy is supposed to do.

When I was very young and first seeing Fields in films, I think I recognized that it was great comedy. I do know for a fact that I liked it, but at the same time I was embarrassed by my tastes. Those were generally genteel and self-consciously very serious times. So Fields — along with Laurel & Hardy, and the Marx Brothers — was considered some king of an animated potboiler. (I was for many years embarrassed, also, by the fact that I didn't like opera. I still don't like opera, but I'm no longer embarrassed about it.) Today I'm comforted by the fact that I was right about Fields. The man was a consummate artist. I think it's great that people are again flocking to see those old films of his.

For my own part, I suppose I am a little awed now to think that I'm considered somewhat of an expert on Fields. I'm not an expert; I just happen to love the guy's attitude toward life and the way he went about living it in whatever role he was playing. The nature of my work offers me considerable exposure and because I respond to no request faster than the one to do a Fields bit, even a throwaway line, I suppose I might as well accept the fact that I've been a little responsible, in one way or another, for getting people interested in Fields.

When someone said to me, "How does it feel to carry the responsibility of being the coach of a cult?" I answered, mustering my best Fieldsian dialect, "Ah yes, my dear, the road to the top is craggy!"

"I Never Met Fields Except in the Dark"

by Richard F. Shepard

cultural news reporter of The New York Times

IT'S A Golden Age of Quotations we are living through. No movement can hope to succeed unless somebody has had something to say about it. Platitudes, pungent and puerile, abound, awaiting selection, to order, by the browser in ideas who is out to find a Founding Father, with appropriately fitting aphorisms, for some going philosophy. The *New York Times* runs a quote-of-the-day, assuring us that somebody always has something to say about something, regardless of how trivial the matter is. Mankind may be running out of time, patience and prerogatives but it is not running out of words.

Relevance. Involvement. Commitment. W. C. Fields. There's a bit of an anti-sequitur in there, no? The first three are catchwords of our time, the new "good words" that drag people away from navel-contemplation and enmesh them in causes that will, it is hoped, disturb some people for the benefit of others. These new words have replaced other "bad" words such as conformity, patriotism, concern, faith, which also roused people from non-lethal lethargy to conditions of euphoria that usually ended in misery and bloodshed.

But — Fields? What has he to do with all these catchwords of conflict? What does he have to say that's relevant, or — worse — involved, or, — heaven help us, — committed? Does he speak to youth from the grave, an ancient oracle competing for customers with the I Ching? Never mind youth for a minute: can Fields pep up the older generation? Did he ever meet a payroll? Well, you're certainly looking for a lot in a forward that is not even prefacing such a known moral commodity as Ralph Waldo Emerson. But, every journey of a single mile starts wtih a thousand opinions. I strongly suggest that you let the words of the immortal card, so cunningly compiled in these pages, serve as the jumping off spot for your own conclusions. Start moving to the rear of the book, please.

Fields was an actor, not a philosopher. He was a juggler, an entertainer of the low-type who gave interviews in which he never let the world know that his stuff really boasted a deep *weltanschauung* behind its tawdry, simple slapstick. Actors who think big usually don't amount to much, and actors who become political leaders amount to even less, even when they become Governors.

Fields made 40 films, many of them real dogs by current critical standards. He was the kind of actor who always played himself — indeed, he wrote most of his own stuff under the names of Charles Bogle, Mahatma Kane Jeeves, Otis Cribblecoblis. He made his bundle in Hollywood and was a sour man of parochial outlooks and unbelievable prejudices. He would have thrown stones at anyone who dared to worship at his altar, which was probably a long mahogany bar fronted with a yellow footrail and brass spittoons and backed by an array of all leading brands.

Now all this is not by way of knocking Fields down. It is just a warning that it would be as ridiculous to sanctify him as it would be to start a cult based on the belief that he walked on whiskey. Fields was a flawed human and let he — or him — who is not, cast the first empty bottle.

But he was always his own man — and here we get to the inspirational, build-this-guy-up business — who had no illusions about the world, although he may have had some about himself. He was a genuinely funny performer with a pug-nose, a chunky silhouette, an ungainly, yet not graceless, gait and a caustic tongue that wagged savagely on and off the screen and is the entire reason we are dealing with him at all. His lines were designed to get laughs, not to sway masses. His thoughts were simple and phrased in words that would not confuse the toddlers who jammed the Saturday afternoon matinee to see someone who sincerely hated them.

Fields delivered his stuff in a voice that varied much as four-tone Mandarin does, usually ending his utterances in a trailing-off rising inflection. He was a dominating figure who started out as a juggler and a bit of a clown and maintained both talents during his movie career.

He was born in 1891 as Claude William Dukinfield to a poor family in Philadelphia. His ambition was to become a comic juggler, which he had achieved as W. C. Fields by the time he was 19. He worked his way to Hollywood from vaudeville, by way of seven seasons with the Ziegfeld Follies. He was married once, but it lasted only until they separated seven years later. He had one son, who is as even-keeled in the business world today as his father was a-list in show business. Fields died in 1946. End of biography.

His movie titles included *The Bank Dick, It's a Gift, My Little Chickadee, International House, If I Had a Million, David Copperfield,* and a string of others that spanned more than 20 years of grinding cameras. He worked with Marion Davies, Chester Conklin, Charles Ruggles, Marlene Dietrich, Mae West, and Orson Welles, to drop a few names.

Enough of this harping on facts. A mere listing of events and putting Fields into a context of motion picture greatness are chores for certificated cinematologists and critics. Besides, facts and figures are tricky — some fellow you don't know has already been working for three years on a doctoral thesis that will knock your purported data into the dead-letter office. A critical evaluation of Fields the comic against Chaplin the comic merely elicits letters from students who are out to demolish you — fine for a periodical that can fill future issues with free contributions in the form of a mailbag, but useless in a book which does not anticipate a follow-up riposte edition. The publisher will be very happy to sell out current stock.

But it is my job here to root out a message for the reader — to edify or educate, to show how the following pages of past quotes mean something now. There are the forewords written from personal reminiscence: "I first saw W. C. Fields in Beverly Hills at a D. W. Griffith garden party. . . ." But that's impossible, because I never met Fields except in the dark, he on the screen and I on my seat. Then there's a contextual gambit: "In a world brinking on destruction, W. C. Fields must shine as a beacon on a safe and happy shore recalling us to yesterday's. . . ." Also impossible; Fields didn't shine, he glowered.

This doesn't mean that we must look at Fields as a disembodied artifact, a lately turned-up Dead Sea Scroll. The highest critical commendation of a work of art today is that it is "honest," that it doesn't have a shred of "sentiment." That's our boy, all the way from 30 years ago. "Dr. Strangelove" needed a plot and fantasy to make its devastating comment on the fallibity of human nature. Black comedy pulverizes us with smashing humor that underscores hopelessness. Sometimes, it seems, these newcomers are really softies, do-gooders frightening us into mending our ways.

But when Fields said, "A thing worth having is worth cheating for," he was not being subtly hortatory. He meant it. He regarded humanity as a menace, some species of it more menacing than others. He never tired of exposing the most mild nudnick as a potential threat to the next man's peace of mind. He was cruel, which is what honestly often comes down to, and intolerant, which is something honesty often ends up as. He was funny, which is something honesty is often not. At least these are the characteristics of Fields on film and in public comment.

He distrusted, even disliked women. In *My Little Chickadee*, he brags about having knocked down some troublesome harridan. When he is reminded that somebody else knocked her down, he mutters, proudly, "Well, I was the one that started kicking her." His screen wives are almost always Xantippes, pushing him on to self-improvement, financial gain and social advancement. It should be noted here, abruptly, that for all of his dour ambience, Fields is rarely the strong character in his movies: he is more an irascible star to whom things happen, things that confirm his misanthropy.

But, wait, don't get him wrong. I nearly forgot that we live in a time when homosexuality and other sexual innovations are served up as routinely as the salad on a table d'hote menu. His abhorrence for females only referred to having them around as equal people; as sex, they were probably the best thing available for a man.

Fields' passion for Mae West is hinted at, with magnificent understatement, in *My Little Chickadee*. He wants her, he has the urge — it's all there in the record — but he clearly doesn't propose to make a hotheaded fool out of himself about it. He makes a fool, but not hotheaded, and there's the big difference. His entire film career toys with the relationship of man and woman, its indispensability and its utter frustration. No making big music on the tenement roof or tumbling in and out of illicit beds. No. Fields is the synthesis of every ordinary man who appreciates a well-turned ankle but never seems to carry it off very well. Man, that's realism. Recommended for adults only.

Children. No child ever came out sweet in a Fields film, at least not to Fields. And this overlapped the Shirley Temple craze era, too. "No man who hates children can be all bad," he is credited as saying, although where and when is somewhat obscure. But, on the other hand, who else would make such a statement? Field's film life was a constant battle with kids, and he was the good guy, never doubt it.

In *It's a Gift,* Fields really comes smack up against a heavy, Baby LeRoy, the adorable moppet, the idol of millions of heaving maternal bosoms. Yet Fields alone in filmdom can cast Baby LeRoy as a heavy, a Little League Genghis Khan. Here is Fields, a harried shopkeeper, not so much crusty as worried, just trying to get through a quietly harrowing day in one piece. And here Baby LeRoy, left by a haughty woman customer in the care of Fields' assistant. Before the malicious minusscule rogue makes a move, Fields diagnoses disaster, an automatically correct conclusion with toddlers, moreso if they don't belong to you. Our hero wastes no time in burbled platitudes and hypocritical cooing. "Get him out!" he shouts immediately, "Get him out of here!" They don't, and in the twinkling of an exposure, Baby LeRoy has turned the faucet on the molasses barrel, flooding the floor and setting the scene for the predictable mama to storm in, criticize Fields for miring her heir in treacle and cancel her custom. Sticky stuff but not sticky sentiment. Fields knew how the baby bounces.

Fields' detestation of the so-called weaker sex, of the tender-aged, extended to all who might conceivably lay claim to our pity. He saw the dog as a crutch to man's ego and not half so exhilarating as drink. In one film, a blind, somewhat deaf man becomes the instrument of humor — Fields is really the butt — as the blind man and his cane become grim reapers of glassware and leave the premises a classic portrait of breakage. The old codger is no one to weep for and, as he stands in midstreet, traffic rushing past him in toro-like sweeps, you cannot be sure that Fields will not script him off to the mortuary before the end of the scene.

It is as though Fields is telling us something. Don't trust these people who can't take care of themselves. If you give in to sentiment, you'll be saddled with them forever. Not a Brotherhood Week sentiment, perhaps, but what could be more selfless than the eternal battle to take care of No. 1. The characters he jousts with are not evil monsters. They are the everyday pests most people have learned to accommodate themselves to, the real petty tyrants dictating the little fellow's life-flow. The milkman rattling the bottles in the morning, the noisy fruit vendor, the road hog, the bureaucrat. They don't even wear an artistic face of evil in Fields films — they are themselves and none the better for it, either.

But don't think for one moment that Fields was merely a dissident agin-er. He was agin many things, including religion, but he loved liquor. He drank in private life and kept the bibulous faith in his screen vehicles. Sobriety was, for him, a dubious virtue. Drink was a challenge to self-control. He was self-controlled, at least he has never shown up as a hopeless self-pitying alcoholic for all that he portrayed himself as a drinker. If anyone had been rash enough to help him with his "problem" Fields probably would have belted them with a bung starter. No, Fields was not an entirely negative man. When he favored a positive aspect, he would pursue it all the way.

Fields not only liked strong drink, he liked strong language. He was able to portray love of liquor on the screen but — in keeping with the paradox of Puritanism that is our society —he could not demonstrate on film any passion for profanity. Before any young freedom-monger charges cop-out, let it be remembered that such a master of virility as Ernest Hemingway, in the more liberal medium of print and writing at a date when Fields had passed his peak, only obscenitied in thy mother's milk without any more brashness than that. But Fields had his own formula, one that any fan soon learned how to interpret. When the moment came for the use of a four-letter expletive, Fields would utter, "DRAT!" obviating the need for anything more vulnerable to the censor. Instead of "Goddamn" Fields came close with "Godfrey Daniels!".

Now, was there ever a man more suited to our period? This emancipated age has unleashed ambition among the ordinary and low-born mortals who climb the backs of others shouting causes and reeking competence. There was a time when you knew the bad guys. Today it can be anybody, even you. We call the special system we contend with the Establishment. Everyman has his own Establishment, whether at the office, in the civil rights movement, in the neighborhood (the landlord, the next-doors who insist you keep your grass as green as theirs), in political parties, in the executive hierachy, in the labor union ranks. The most apathetic citizen is singled out as part of the Establishment by virtue of his passivity and slated for extermination.

Is it any wonder that Fields speaks to the last elements of a free society, the people who seek liberty to make their own mistakes, their own decisions without getting a consensus from family, friends and fellow members. Be on your guard, Fields is telling us. He knows for whom the bell tolls. It is being rung by somebody who wants you to do something, who is going to complain to you about something, who is going to borrow money. Yes, my friend, Fields is announcing that the bell tolls for you — but don't bother him with your troubles. He's got his own.

" The outlandish news that I have gone on the water wagon was dis~ closed recently in the public prints. This, I must sadly confess, is at least partly true. . . . . . .

… But the news has resulted in a vicious rumor being circulated, and I feel it should be nipped at once. The rumor is that, having given up alcohol, I am about to acquire a dog. This is a scoundrelly lie…

... I have not changed my position about either whiskey or dogs. I am in favor of one and against the other...

"There comes a time in the affairs of man when he must take the bull by the tail and face the situation."

... Simply because I don't at the moment imbibe alcohol does not mean I have lost my awareness of alcohol's limit-

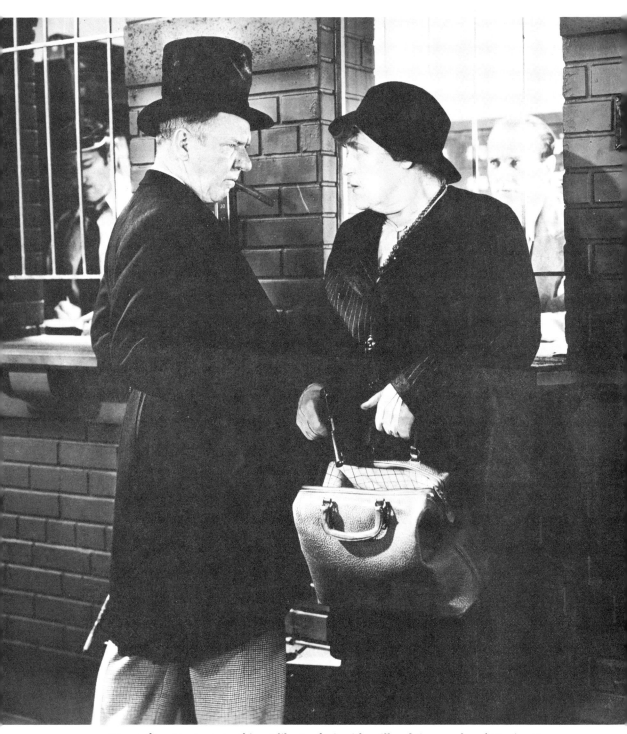

"According to you everything I like to do is either illegal, immoral or fattening."

**less virtues... I do not, in fact, con-
sider I am on the water wagon. I
never drink water...**

"Suffering sciatica — Water!"

...I drink lemonade-straight...

"I never smoked a cigarette until I was nine."

... Alcohol, of course, can take care of itself – which is more than a dog can do...

"I'd rather have two girls at 21 each than one girl at 42."

"I'll knock 'em for a row of lib-labs."

... The fact that alcohol rarely evokes public

praise is a tribute to its own astuteness. . .

"I was in love with a beautiful blonde once — she drove me to drink —
'tis the one thing I'm indebted to her for."

...But through the years the dog has come in for so much praise that I feel constrained to put in a few equally kind and more deserved words for the demon rum...

. . . It is only just and fitting that alcohol should have a few pats on the back. . .

"Once you've got a man seated,
you've got him at your mercy."

. . . Why, if dogs had ever taken the pounding that's been handed out to John Barleycorn, dogs would long ago have sunk into the tongueless silence of the dreamless dust, as Bob Ingersoll put it. . .

"I hope she doesn't get too violent, I haven't spent enough to knock her down."

"I'll be sober tomorrow, but you'll be crazy the rest of your life."

I have spent
forty-two years
closely observing
the beneficent
influences of
alcohol, and
spreading the
good word. Some
of my friends
have been kind
enough to say
that my toil in
the vineyards has
not been in vain...

"...ourth of July —
...was good enough for
...orge Washington, it's
...od enough for me."

...I am sure this is true. My campaign on behalf of alcohol, I hope, has helped in some measure to erase many popular misconceptions about the relative merits of whiskey and dogs...

**...It is a pleasure to report that at last
I am seeing the happy dawn of truth
lighting the world...**

"Things happened!"

.. The wise and intelligent are coming belatedly to realize that alcohol, and not the dog, is man's best friend. Rover is taking a beating – and he should...

The responsibility for this crusade has weighed heavily upon my shoulders. Many times I have felt I was a lone voice crying in the wilderness – an arid wilderness populated by sagebrush, bluenoses and dogs...

"I can lick my weight in wildflowers."

...At such gruesome moments I would solace myself with thoughts of the wondrous gifts of alcohol, the manna that mankind so seldom appreciates....

"I'm beginning to see footprints of a foul conspiracy."

"Beer flowing thru the estate over your grandmother's paisley shawl . . ."

... **Then I would let my voice really cry out in all its power and glory. I would cry, "Set 'em up again!" ..**

"Somehow, Satan
got behind me."

41

... Possibly you have noted the various epithets that have been gratuitously tossed at alcohol. I have used a few myself, such as demon rum, etc....

"A man who overindulges lives in a dream. He becomes conceited. He thinks the whole world revolves around him — and it usually does."

...But the hard names applied to hard liquor are as nothing compared with the loathsome sobriquets used on dogs...

"A thing worth having is worth cheating for."

43

"He's as crooked as a dog's hind leg."

... Canines have become synonymous with all that is low and mean, as witness "you dirty dog," "yellow dog," "I wouldn't do that to a dog," "a dog's life," "he dogged it," "It shouldn't happen to a dog," "doggone it ," etc...

... Surely all these historic phrases cannot be the result of pure chance. There must be some essence of verity in them...

"Women are like
elephants to me.
I like to look at them,
but I wouldn't want
to own one."

"It is impossible to find twelve fair men in all the world."

...And there is. The public has accepted them because it realizes the justice of the obloquies...

... But I have a sneaking hunch that the phrases were coined by a series of true scholars and basic thinkers, and I hereby doff my skimmer to them...

"I'd hardly quit liquor, before I got the d.t.'s. I'd see men with whiskers and high hats, sitting on bulls, and they'd charge me. They almost got me one afternoon."

. . . They wanted to sneak in a good word for alcohol but knew they couldn't succeed if they were too bold about it. So what did they do? They rightly concluded that a few words against dogs would further the case for alcohol. . . . . . That reminds me – send up another case, bartender. And I don't mean dogs. . .

"Somebody put too many olives in my martini last night."

"I feel as though the Russian army had been walking over my
tongue in their stocking feet."

... Going from the ridiculous to the sub-lime, all history is filled with un-solicited tributes to alcohol and the merited vilification of dogs. A glance at reference books is enlightening...

"I oughta write a book:
THE ART OF ARISING
THE MORNING AFTER."

"My little rocky mountain canary."

... **Is it just accidental that alcohol and the alimentary canal are both closely allied and similarly named? Hardly...**

... The ancients knew what they wanted. The Standard American Encyclopedia says in part about alcohol: "Pure

"Keep your hands off my lunch, will you!"

ethyl alcohol has a pleasing ethereal odor and is colorless. It boils at 78.3 degrees.".. .

"My best friend died of drinking too much water. His was
a case of internal drowning."

"Remember, a dead fish can float downstream, but it takes a
live one to swim upstream."

... No dog has these admirable qualities, except as to the lack of color. A dog is the most colorless object in all na-

"Hold your breath and lie down."

ture, and it's time he was told about it. What is a dog, anyway? Simply an antidote for an inferiority complex...

...We order him around, tell him to sit up, lie down, roll over, and all manner of other useless maneuvers, simply to show bystanders that we can

boss something. No man is boss in his own home, but he can make up for it, he thinks, by making a dog play dead. . .

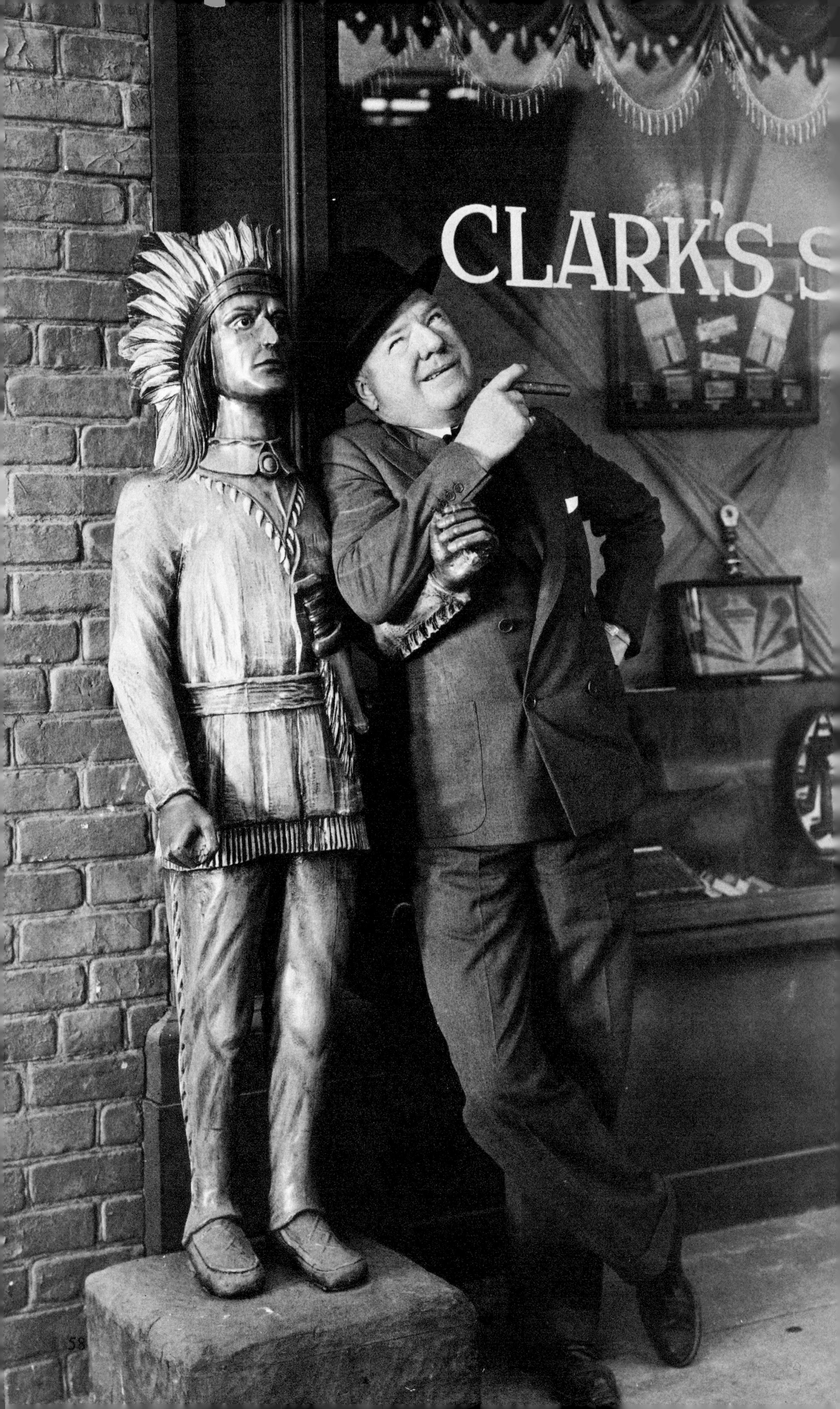
CLARK'S S

...How much better it would be if he had the courage to take a drink and then stand up for his rights...

. . . Even on a hunting trip, supposedly
the supreme office of a dog, whiskey
occupies a more important spot than
he does. And on a fishing trip, where
a dog isn't allowed at all, whiskey
is obviously more indispensable than
fish. . .

"Hold your temper-count 10 — Now let 'er go, you've got a good aim."

"Don't forget — Lady Godiva put everything she had on a horse.'

.. On fox hunts, what is the final ritual?
Calling out the dogs? Not at all. It is
the stirrup cup. . .

...The hounds mill around impatiently while their masters bid a reluctant farewell to alcohol...

I am convinced that the reason fox-hunters ride at top speed across the

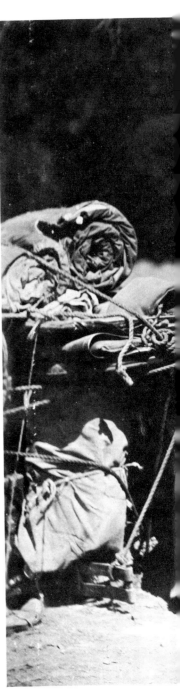

"Get away from me you little bastard! For two cents — or even one — I'd kick in your teeth!"

meadows is because they want to be rid of dogs, foxes and the rest of the silly business and get back to their drinking as quickly as they can. Hunting! Pshaw!...

"If I didn't have an accident I'd never gotten here."

"What a splendid view of California climate."

...The whole theory of foxhunting is plainly just an excuse to take a drink...

...What can you do with a fox even if you happen to catch one?...

"I know a thief when I see one. When I was young I was the biggest thief at large. I'd steal golf balls, piggy banks of dear little kiddies, or nozzles off the hoses of the rectory lawn — anything and everything. Then, when I got into the chips myself and had plenty of dough, my character changed. From then on there was nothing I hated worse than a thief."

... Very little. For all practical purposes he is as worthless as a dog... Instead of the historic post of m.f.h. – master of fox hounds – the hunters would be more honest and more to the point if they had an m.o.a. – master of alcohol – in charge of the fusty and tiresome affair...

"How could you hurt anybody, throwing them on their head?"

"I may be a liar, but at least I'm a gentleman."

"Any man who hates children can't be all bad."

T.N.T. DANGER

68

...I recall once seeing a dog chew on a little kid, which is not in itself a bad idea.......but it does show a dog's intentions...

"I'm like Robin Hood — I take from the rich and give to the poor — us poor."

... Well, sir, a dog lover witnessing the demonstration was heard to remark, "My, my, that poor dog must have been terribly hungry." ... There's a dog lover for you...

"I HATE YOU."

"Shades of Bacchus."

... **On another occasion I was caught in a snowstorm in the virgin forests of sunny California. A rescue dog approached through the drifts and hovered over me...**

"I think I can do something with it . . . don't know what yet."

...I undid the bottle of brandy from around the beast's neck, whereupon he promptly bit my hand, grabbed the bottle and drank the contents himself...

...He turned out to be a lap dog, and I don't mean from Lapland...

"You perfidious loud-mouthed etcetera, the only thing I'm grateful for is that you've driven me to drink."

"She hasn't been unwrapped yet."

...Among other things, you have to train a dog. But you never have to train a bottle of grog...

"I don't know why I ever come in here — the flies
get the best of everything."

... A dog will run up and lick your hand. No bottle will do that......If the whiskey ever starts licking your hand, I would advise you lay off it for awhile, say five or ten minutes...

"There may be some things better than sex, and some things may be worse. But there is nothing exactly like it."

... We frequently hear of people dying from too much drinking...That this happens is a matter of record. But the blame almost always is placed on whiskey...

"The bottle is mightier than the quiver."

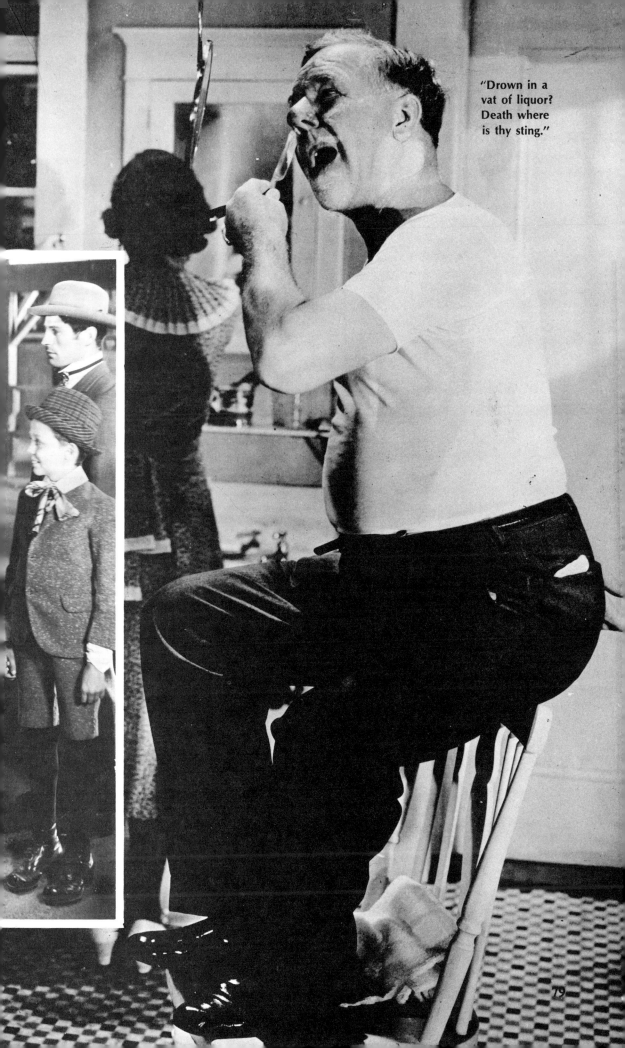

"Drown in a vat of liquor? Death where is thy sting."

... Why this should be I never could understand. You can die from drinking too much of anything – coffee, water, milk, soft drinks and all such stuffs as that...

"'This place was supposed to be a saloon but the censor cut it out.'"

... And so long as the presence of death lurks with anyone who goes through the simple act of swallowing, I will make mine whiskey. No water, thank you...

...Whiskey is admitted everywhere – well, practically everywhere. But dogs are barred from many places such as cafes, stores, restaurants,

"Please don't call me Mr. — it's so formal, call me
Marc Anthony . . . Marc for short."

**hotels and certain passenger trains...
Dogs and whiskey have one thing in
common and that is the matter of
housebreaking...**

"Tell my wife not to wait up for me tonight because I won't be
home for a month."

... A dog that is not housebroken frequently creates tragic interludes. But dropping a bottle of whiskey in the house and breaking it brings about crises no less tragic...
Who has not experienced the unutterable despair that follows the crash of a treasured bottle?...

"Never mind what I tell you to do — do what I tell you."

"DRAT!"

"I should have gone to night school, then I'd be able to add."

... **There is no question as to whether whiskey or the dog is man's best friend. When two kindred souls get together for a friendly session, do they sit there and pet dogs?** ...

...Well, they don't in any of the circles with which I have graced my humble presence...

"I'm a broadminded man — gads,
I don't object to nine aces in one deck.
But when a man has five aces in one hand —
And I dealt myself four aces —
    And besides that,
I know what I dealt him . . ."

...Can a man have both whiskey and dogs? Certainly. A man can have many loves...

"I shall rehearse you in your line."

...He can love whiskey, dogs, cigars, horses and his secretary, to mention only a few...

"My heart is a bargain today. Will you take me?"

. . . Happily, not many men are ever compelled to make a choice among the things they love. But if any man were faced with the necessity, say, of giving up either dogs or whiskey, which do you think he would do? . . .

"If at first you don't succeed, try, try again. Then quit.
No use being a damn fool about it."

"All dressed up like a well-kept grave."

...I won't bother to answer that one...

... **The advantages of whiskey over dogs are legion. Whiskey does not need to be periodically wormed, it does not need to be fed, it never requires a special kennel, it has no toenails to**

"I always talk loud: I'm a sheriff."

be clipped or coat to be stripped. Whiskey sits quietly in its special nook until you want it. True, whiskey has a nasty habit or running out, but then so does a dog...

"Goodness gracious, the river's rising."

"I note the derogatory rumors concerning my use of alcoholic stimulants and lavish living. It is the penalty of greatness . . ."

...Dog lovers like to point out that the friendship of a dog gives his master self-confidence and happiness. Possibly this is so...

... **How a mauling from a mastiff can make a guy feel heroic is beyond me, but for the sake of argument I will admit it...**

"I'll bend every effort to win ... and I come from a long line
of effort benders."

... **But it is a well-known fact that whiskey likewise gives one an heroic feeling. A slight amount makes every man his own Napoleon. Now, if dogs and whiskey can both make you a hero, why not take whiskey?** ...

"Every cloud has a silver lining and every plate of vegetable soup is filled with vegetables."

"I never drank anything stronger than gin before breakfast."

... I remember one day working on location up at Malibu Lake – more water!

...I was working with that Trojan infant Baby LeRoy. My mission was to carry him on my arm past the camera. Baby LeRoy's emoting in that scene consisted of looking at the camera. I had him on my arm. The rubberized diaper hadn't been invented. Every time the little nipper saw the camera it almost scared the kidneys out of him...

... We took the scene over and over again for hours on end. They gave the child a drink of water of all things. They gave him his milk bottle. He tried to conk me with it. I ducked...

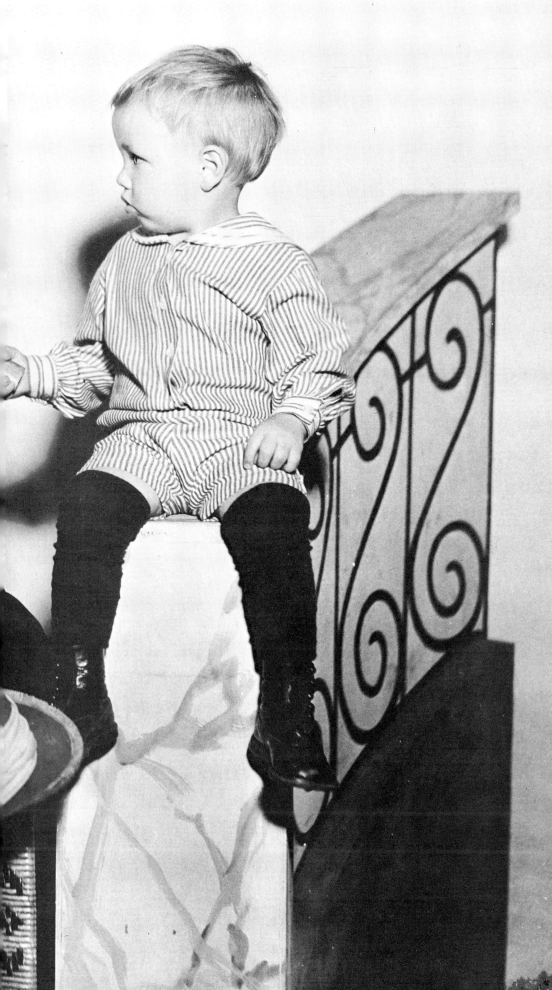

...I told his nurse to get me a racing form and I would play nurse until she returned. I quietly removed the nipple from Baby LeRoy's bottle, dropped in a couple of noggins of gin, and returned to Baby LeRoy. After sucking on the pacifier for a few minutes, he staggered through the scene like a Barrymore."

Fields used a verbal drill
on Charlie McCarthy in
the celebrated feud of 1938.

Even in dictating a short note, Fields could not stay long with the niceties of propriety.

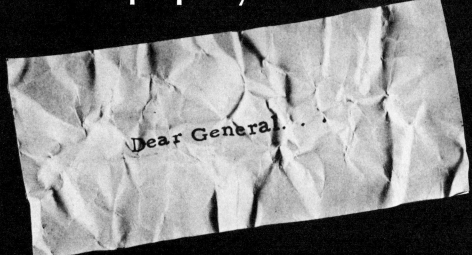

Dear General . . .

No, that's too friendly. .

My dear General . . .

Still too friendly.

General Wagonall. . .
Dear Sir. . .

Now, why should I
be so respectful?
I'll demote the pup!

Corporal Wagonall. . .

Har-ha, he'll resent that.
He'd resent anything
I'd call him, the crud.

Just for that,

Private Wagonall,
put yourself under arrest!

WOMEN HAVE ALWAYS PLAYED...

an important role in the comedy of W. C. Fields. Just as few people think of Fields as a leading man, even fewer remember that he had several leading ladies.

Alison Skipworth (**If I Had a Million, Tillie and Gus**), Peggy Hopkins Joyce (**International House**), Mary Boland (**Six of a Kind**), Zasu Pitts (**Mrs. Wiggs of the Cabbage**

Patch), Martha Raye **(The Big Broadcast of 1938)** and Mae West **(My Little Chickadee),** to name a few.

In most instances Fields was the underdog. Harassed, he had only one defense — his sharp tongue. Mae West, in many ways, epitomized all of Fields' leading ladies. Therefore it is fitting to devote the next few pages to his involvement with her and in doing so utilize quotes uttered by Fields at various times to various women.

"What won't they think of next?"

"Now that I'm here I shall dally in the valley —
and believe me I can dally."

"She's as solid as a brick telephone booth."

"It's the climate. I've been drinking much too much orange juice."

"Don't wait up for me dear, I may play a little parchesi before coming to bed."

"Don't telegraph — WRITE!"

W.C. FIELDS ANNOUNCES...

LOS ANGELES (Calif.) Dec. 8, 1933. W. C. Fields announces that he has been appointed official Santa Claus for Hollywood.

"Seems," explained Felds yesterday in his dressing-room, flicking ashes at a picture of Baby LeRoy, "that the boys and girls around here want me to pass out the presents. Well, sir, a Fields never weakens." He eyed LeRoy's picture, "Now take the kid there. He's the only one in Hollywood who still believes in Santa Claus — or at least will admit it. The first present down on this list is for him. And it's from me."

Fields reached into his dressing-room closet and produced a toy horn with a rubber bulb squeezer.

"See how nicely I've slashed the bulb with a razor?" gloated Fields. "They gave him one that worked in the picture, so this oughta fool him into trying pretty hard. I'll teach him to steal my scenes! And here's a rocking chair that won't rock. That oughta irritate him.

"And, boy, I've figured one from Mae West to Marlene Dietrich. It's a nice photograph of Mae in one of her Gay Nineties outfits. I guess it should make Marlene happy when she finds that in her sock.

"And for Mae West I got a book on fashions, telling how the slim figure is coming back, and how women shouldn't wear diamonds. Mae should be pleased with that."

---

struck where the Democratic Administration was most vulnerable. Evidence of Communist infiltration in the Federal Establishment had definitely appeared, though wildly exaggerated by ...

"International House" brought Fields and socialite Peggy Hopkins Joyce together in several hilarious scenes.

During a ride with Fields in his car, The Spirit of South Brooklyn, Miss Joyce squirmed and complained. Fields stopped the car to see what it was that was disturbing her comfort. "Why," he gravelled, as he picked up a cat from the seat, "It's a little pussy."

Another ride, in a plane, more squirming by Miss Joyce. This time Fields unearthed a batch of kittens from the seat. "I wonder what their parents were," gushed Miss Joyce, to which Fields gave the terse reply: "Careless."

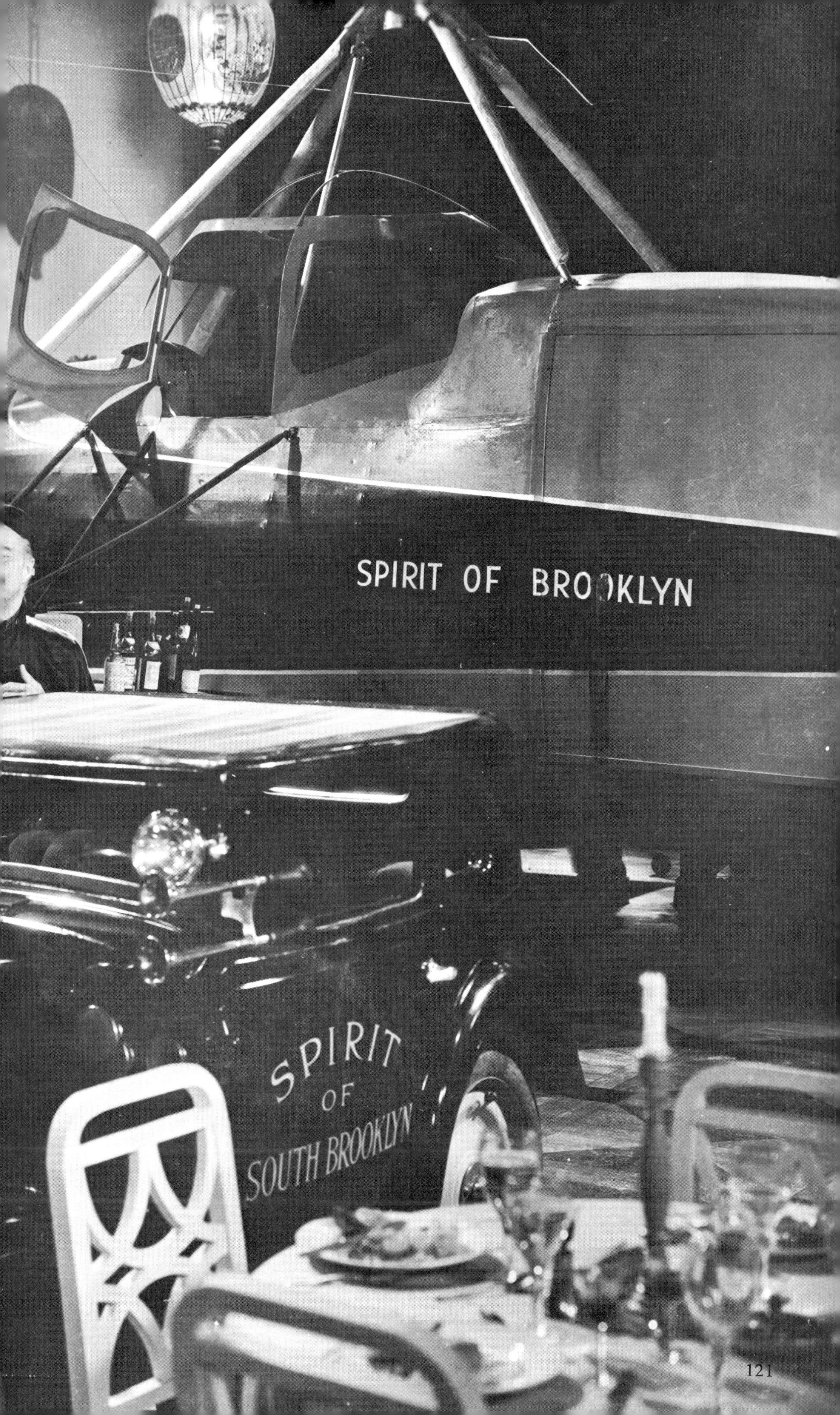
SPIRIT OF BROOKLYN
SPIRIT
OF
SOUTH BROOKLYN

From Boy Juggler to
Star Comedian

written in 1928 by the $5,000-a-week star of the
Earl Carroll "Vanities", W. C. Fields.

RECKONED in monetary terms, I was not a howling success at the beginning of my career. Obsessed with the idea of juggling every conceivable object as a lad, very early I became proficient in this art. In fact I felt sure I was as good as any of the jugglers I saw in the shows around Philadelphia, where I spent my childhood.

So, armed with a lot of nerve, equipped with a lot of juggling practice I sauntered forth in the world at the age of eleven years to dazzle the amusement-seeking public with feats of juggling. I got an engagement at a summer park, through a booking-agent. I'll never forget the name. It was Flynn & Grant's Park, at Norristown, and it was a twenty-five-cent trolley ride from Philadelphia. I was to receive five dollars a week.

I got the five dollars, but I had to pay a dollar and a half commission to the booking-office, and it cost me over four dollars to ride back and forth to the park. I was rooming in a club over a blacksmith shop, and foolishly came into Philadelphia every night to sleep in my old haunt. As a kid I could not reason out that I might have found some place to sleep in the Park. I just got used to sleeping over the shop, and naturally thought I must come back to my room.

I heard there was a demand for talent in Atlantic C.ty, and I went down to that same resort. I was engaged at the Fortesque Pavilion. Frank Tinney was playing a cornet in the place. They had a stage—the old-timers will recall it. You could get a big glass of beer for a nickel, and sit and watch the show while you quaffed your beer. Of course a few people ordered more expensive drinks, but there were times when it was very difficult to keep the pavilion filled. The things we did there were quite laughable as I look back on them.

A favorite way to fill up the place was to work a fake rescue. One of the performers would go out in the surf, pretend to be caught in the undertow, and shout for help. We would all be ready, rush in the water and drag the rescued person into the pavilion. Naturally the crowd followed, and if it was a woman we rescued the crowd was particularly large. Once inside they bought drinks and we were supposed to be entertaining enough to keep them there. It was a great racket, and we got plenty of fun out of it. I received ten dollars and cakes. "Cakes" was an expression of the olden days for eats. We had the privilege of ordering what we wanted to eat several times a day. So that was a little better.

The first time I got away from juggling was in a burlesque show. It was a one-night-stand affair, owned by a man named Jim Fulton. All that bothered Jim was that every time he interested an "angel" in the show to pay the bills, the angel got stuck on his wife. He said it seemed odd to him that with twenty other girls in the show every backer that came along couldn't find somebody else but Mrs. Fulton to be smitten with. I juggled, played a dozen bits, and got a chance to develop a line of humor. Here was another step upward. I got twenty-five dollars a week, but it was rather precarious, and some weeks we did not get salaries.

Fred Irwin, one of the founders of the old-time burlesque wheel, gave me my next job and it was another upward step, for I was engaged at the salary of thirty-five dollars per week. And all I heard from Irwin was that he could never make any money paying me such a big salary. I kicked for a good spot on the bill, claiming I wanted a chance to earn the money. Some critic gave me a big boost. I heard, afterwards, that he never even saw the show. He said I was great. I took his notice with me and called on Irwin for more money. He increased me to fifty dollars a week. I was all over the stage and never had a minute to rest in the show. When I stopped to figure how often I made appearances for that sum I threatened to quit, and Irwin increased me to seventy-five dollars, which I got till the end of the season.

I was singing, clowning, juggling and talking comedy, and kept it right up till now. And still a couple of reviewers passing on my work in the Earl Carroll *Vanities,* wrote as though I had started in the motion pictures and just graduated into the spoken drama. They said they were glad to "discover" I had a voice. So, after all, what difference does it make to the new generation how much you have done, or how much fame you have won?

William Morris dropped back stage one night and gave me some illuminating facts on vaudeville. The next season I was in the varieties at one hundred and twenty-five dollars a week. I figured if I could live long enough I surely could arrive at the five-hundred figure. But times and salaries changed. For several seasons my salary went up and down. I wanted to see the world, and booked for a tour of Europe. I started in Germany, and, of course, had to go back to juggling and pantomime, not knowing the languages of the countries I visited.

In America we hear a great deal about foreigners having a better chance here than in other countries. There is only one time a Yankee has any difficulty in a foreign country, I discovered, and that is right at the time some American boxer or athlete bests a native of the country in which an American happens to be at the time. In London, one time, an Englishman tried to ruin my performance the night some Britisher had been badly beaten over here in a prize fight. I stepped down front and asked the audience not to feel unkindly about my heckler. I told them the thing had happened to me once before, that I had berated the annoyer from the stage, and when I had finished the keeper of an insane asylum came down the aisle and took the poor chap out and back to the institution. The audience appreciated the humor of the thing and laughed my traducer out of countenance.

Vaudeville took me all over the world. I played the Malay Straits, down through India, Australia, to New Zealand and back, through Samoa and India, skirting the coast of Africa. Every winter I came back to America and made a tour or worked in a show.

And if the public envies the performers who draw salary for traveling through those distant Pacific countries, which seem so romantic on paper, let them bear in mind that every journey is a hazard almost equal to a flight across the North Pole.

It was at the famous Koster & Bial's that I made my first bow to a New York audience. It is not necessary to elaborate on the exhilaration which comes to a performer when he steps in front of his first Metropolitan audience. He has reached the pinnacle.

When I played the Orpheum Circuit for Martin Beck I got acquainted with a young humpbacked chap who sold candy and magazines on the trains. Little did I know how he was to help me in later years. When I reached South Africa I received a wire in Natal on the east coast that the theatre in Johannesburg was burned, and not to come there. The Boer War was just over, and a traveler had to have a citizenship card to even purchase a railroad ticket. Here I was with a contract for Johannesburg and unable to reach the place. I was a dejected comedian sitting in a railroad station. A train pulled in, and the first person to jump off was the little candy butcher I had known on the Pacific Coast. He was a Boer. He had a card of citizenship which he loaned me and I got a ticket to Natal. The manager was surprised to see me. I think he had given orders to keep me out of the town. He had to fill my contract, so he rented a hall and gave a show.

Charles B. Dillingham had seen me in *The Ham Tree* with McIntyre & Heath. He appraised me for a rôle in *Watch Your Step* and cabled me an offer to Australia. I spent thirty-nine days reaching the show. We opened in Syracuse, N. Y., and I played three nights, less than one-tenth of the time I consumed in traveling to the engagement. I did not *fit*. But the engagement served one purpose. It kept me in America. Before my contract time with Dillingham expired I was in the *Follies*. Since then it has been one show after another, but always at an increased stipend.

Of course, I could not escape the motion pictures, and here again was a multiplication of salary. I can not and do not expect the legitimate producers to compete in salary with the pictures. But I must say that when I started out in Flynn & Grant's park at five dollars a week that even my boyish imagination never conceived a salary of more than five thousand dollars a week, for any time in my life. Earl Carroll has seen fit to outbid several other producers to that figure for my newly "discovered" voice, so here I am among the *Vanities* beauties, my income multiplied exactly one thousand and forty times since I juggled Indian clubs and rubber balls in the open air for five berries a week, three shows a day, seven days to the week.

I like to look back over the good old days. They were all happy because they are full of promise. But you cannot blame me if I do not sigh for their return.

"Most people have a feeling they are coming back to this life some way, somehow. But me – I know I'm going through only once."

SOURCES OF PHOTOS, ARTICLES AND CAPTIONS IN "DRAT!"

(**P** stands for photo, usually a still from the film indicated; **C** identifies the source of the caption on that page)

17-104		Running commentary of W. C. Fields in large type is taken from his article, "Alcohol and Me" in the October 13, 1942 issue of PIC Magazine, © Copyright, 1942 by Street and Smith Publications, Inc., and excerpted here by permission of the Condé Nast Publications, Inc.
18	P	The Old-Fashioned Way (1934)
19	P	Follow the Boys (1944)
	C	Tille & Gus (1933)
20	P	Tillie & Gus (1933)
	C	Six of a Kind (1934)
21	P	Never Give a Sucker An Even Break (1941)
	C	Mississippi (1935)
22	C	The Bank Dick (1940)
23	P	International House (1932)
24	P	You're Telling Me (1934)
	C	To Come
25	P	Follow the Boys (1944)
	C	Man on Flying Trapeze (1935)
26-27	P	Man on Flying Trapeze (1935)
28	P	Million Dollar Legs (1932)
	C	Never Give a Sucker an Even Break (1941)
29	P	Mrs. Wiggs of the Cabbage Patch (1934)
30	P	Mrs. Wiggs of the Cabbage Patch (1934)
	C	Mississippi (1935)
31	P	Man on Flying Trapeze (1935)
	C	My Little Chickadee (1940)
32-33	P	You Can't Cheat an Honest Man (1939)
32	C	It's A Gift (1934)
34	P	Mississippi (1935)
	C	Tillie & Gus (1933)
35	P&C	Man on Flying Trapeze (1935)
36	P	Poppy (1936)
37	C	Big Broadcast of 1938
38	P	Tillie & Gus (1933)
	C	Six of a Kind (1934)
39	P	Never Give a Sucker an Even Break (1941)
	C	The Bank Dick (1940)
41	P	You're Telling Me (1934)
	C	Man on Flying Trapeze (1935)
42	P	Never Give a Sucker an Even Break (1941)
	C	Newspaper interview
43	P	Million Dollar Legs (1932)
	C	My Little Chickadee (1940)
44	P	The Bank Dick (1940)
	C	Tillie & Gus (1933)
45	P	You Can't Cheat an Honest Man (1939)
	C	Mississippi (1935)
46	P	Tillie & Gus (1933)
	C	Newspaper interview
47	P	You Can't Cheat an Honest Man (1939)
	C	Newspaper interview

48	P	International House (1932)
	C	Never Give a Sucker an Even Break (1941)
49	P	Never Give a Sucker an Even Break (1941)
	C	Six of a Kind (1934)
50	P	The Bank Dick (1940)
	C	My Little Chickadee (1940)
51	P	You Can't Cheat an Honest Man (1939)
	C	The Old-Fashioned Way (1934)
52	P	My Little Chickadee (1940)
	C	You Can't Cheat an Honest Man (1939)
53	P	Mrs. Wiggs of the Cabbage Patch (1934)
	C	Newspaper interview
54	P	Man on Flying Trapeze (1935)
	C	Mississippi (1935)
55	P	Six of a Kind (1934)
	C	International House (1932)
56-57	P	Man on Flying Trapeze (1935)
58	P	You're Telling Me (1934)
59	P	Man on Flying Trapeze (1935)
	C	My Little Chickadee (1940)
60	P	My Little Chickadee 1940)
	C	Never Give a Sucker an Even Break (1941)
61	P	Never Give a Sucker an Even Break (1941)
	C	Tillie & Gus (1933)
62	P	Mrs. Wiggs of the Cabbage Patch (1934)
	C	Fields to autograph hounds
63	P	It's a Gift (1934)
	C	Never Give a Sucker an Even Break (1941)
64	P	If I Had a Million (1932)
	C	Never Give a Sucker an Even Break (1941)
65	P	The Bank Dick (1940)
	C	Newspaper interview
66	P	My Little Chickadee (1940)
	C	Man on Flying Trapeze (1935)
67	P	The Old-Fashioned Way (1934)
	C	Newspaper interview
68	P	Publicity shot (1934)
	C	Attribution
69	P	You're Telling Me (1934)
	C	Poppy (1936)
70	P	Million Dollar Legs (1932)
	C	It's a Gift (1934)
71	P	You Can't Cheat an Honest Man (1939)
72	P	My iLttle Chickadee
	C	It's a Gift (1934)
73	P	Big Broadcast of 1938
	C	Never Give a Sucker an Even Break (1941)
74	P	My Little Chickadee (1940)
	C	Newspaper interview
75	P	You Can't Cheat an Honest Man (1939)

PHOTO CREDITS

Photos from the following Paramount Features are reproduced through the courtesy of MCA-TV: If I Had a Million, Million Dollar Legs, International House, Tillie & Gus, Six of a Kind, You're Telling Me, Mrs. Wiggs of the Cabbage Patch, It's a Gift, The Old-Fashioned Way, Mississippi, Man on the Flying Trapeze, Poppy, Big Broadcast of 1938.

Photos from the following Universal Features are reproduced through the courtesy of Universal Pictures Corporation: You Can't Cheat an Honest Man, The Bank Dick, My Little Chickadee, Never Give a Sucker an Even Break, Follow the Boys.